The Life

Multistate Bar Exam Practice Questions & Answers

Printed in the United States of America

ISBN: 9798803557609

This book is a general review of legal subjects for the Multistate Bar Exam. This book is not intended as a source for advice regarding legal matters.

Table of Contents

Practice Questions...1

Answers...123

Question 1

Erica and Lisa began arguing one evening at a birthday party. The argument escalated into a physical altercation between the two women. Multiple party attendees assisted with stopping the fight, but only after Erica hit Lisa in the face with a wine bottle. After the fight was over, Erica walked to her car while Lisa yelled, "I'll be at your house tonight, bitch." Lisa had a reputation of robbing drug dealers with a shotgun. Erica was scared and decided to follow Lisa when she left the lounge. As Lisa approached a traffic light, Erica pulled up next to her, brandished a pistol and fired eight times before speeding away.

Can Erica claim self-defense?

(A) Yes, because Erica feared that Lisa would jeopardize her safety.

(B) No, because Erica's conduct was an unnecessary and over-reactive response to Lisa's threat.

(C) No, because Erica did not face a direct threat concerning fear for her life.

(D) Yes, because Lisa's history of harming others and a near-future attack from Lisa was predictable.

Notes

Question 2

Kevin was a master thief of exquisite art and his skill-set was in great demand. Kevin hired Sam to build a walk-in safe for his basement. Although Sam was very experienced, he habitually ate on the job and never cleaned up after himself. Kevin saw Sam leaving food wrapping paper on the floor one day and he confronted Sam about it. Consequently, Sam assigned all of his remaining work for the walk-in safe to a friend, who was a licensed contractor. Sam occasionally came by the job site to examine his friend's work. Kevin did not mind the work being performed by Sam's friend. Three weeks later, Sam's friend stopped showing up for work and neither Sam nor Kevin could reach the friend by phone or email.

Who is responsible for finishing Kevin's walk-in safe?

  (A) Sam and the new contractor.

  (B) Sam's friend, the contractor, is liable for all damages caused by his default and will be partially responsible for the loss that Sam will incur, based on a divisible contract concept.

  (C) Sam is responsible because, not for his assignment to the new contractor, Kevin would avoid all legal damages.

  (D) Sam is responsible because the assignment to the new contractor was not in writing.

Notes

Question 3

Congress recently passed a law that banned federal funding of any sort for states that approve the use and sale of ghost guns. State Q was a pro-gun state, which is where Butch lived and owned a gun shop. Butch had a reputation for selling large amounts of altered ghost guns, and many of the weapons were traced to cold-case murders. Butch submitted an application in hopes of receiving federal funding, which would pay for a gun safety class that he offered to women and senior citizens. During a recent election, state Q voters passed a referendum that allowed ghost guns to be owned by citizens who were not convicted felons.

Because the state now allows the use and sale of ghost guns, can Butch receive federal funding for the gun safety class?

(A) Yes, because the Tenth Amendment prohibits Congress from commandeering the states.

(B) No, because Congress is permitted to deny federal funds based on legislation.

(C) Yes, because interstate commerce is not involved in this situation, and the Tenth Amendment allows the states to exercise police powers.

(D) No, because all legislation passed by Congress will generally be supported by the supremacy clause, which is also authorized by the General Welfare Clause.

Notes

Question 4

Pam and Samantha owned a golf course as joint tenants and they lived on the property. Samantha was growing bothered with Pam's weekly loud parties, which included millionaires and exotic dancers. Samantha believed the parties included drugs and prostitution. One day a heated argument erupted between Samantha and Pam. Samantha threatened to tell the police about Pam's private parties. Pam threatened to kill Samantha if she ever spoke to the police concerning the parties. The next day Samantha met with an attorney who created a will for her. Samantha's will devised all of her possessions and her share of the golf course to a nephew who lived in another state. Two days later, Samantha's body was discovered in a park and her death was ruled to be a homicide, based on the cause of death, which was strangulation.

What will be the outcome regarding Samantha's will?

(A) The devise to Samantha's nephew will supersede all prior rights concerning Samantha's assets and her interest in the golf course.

(B) The devise to Samantha's nephew will supersede all prior rights concerning her share of the golf course.

(C) Pam's right of survivorship supersedes Samantha's devise regarding the golf course.

(D) The joint tenancy became null and void due to the creation and devise of Samantha's will.

Notes

Question 5

Yolanda was in federal custody after being arrested for gun and drug charges. When agents executed a search warrant at her apartment they discovered several rounds of ammunition, devices used to make ghost guns, two altered M16 machine guns and counterfeit social security cards. While Yolanda was being held on these charges, she was also charged with committing 50 robberies at local retail stores. During each robbery, surveillance footage captured the suspect wearing tennis shoes with a pink trim at the front of their shoe. At trial for these robberies, the prosecution wanted to introduce evidence to prove that Yolanda wore tennis shoes with a pink trim during her arrest. However, the defense attorney timely objected to the introduction of such evidence.

Will the Court sustain the objection?

   (A) Yes, because other acts must be proven beyond a reasonable doubt.

   (B) Yes, because admitting this evidence would involve prejudicial effects which outweigh its probative value.

   (C) No, because such evidence is rationally acceptable.

   (D) No, because this evidence reflects the modus operandi of the suspect.

Notes

Question 6

Christine was being sued by her business partner regarding restrictive covenant violations and trade secret misappropriation. Her attorney was going through a divorce and he was also being investigated for the production of child pornography in a different state. The plaintiff filed a complaint and Christine's attorney timely filed an answer. Just beyond 22 days, Christine met with her attorney and the topic of damages and requesting a jury trial were discussed. The attorney was indicted two days ago, and he filed a motion for a jury trial in Christine's case on the following day.

Will the Court grant the motion for a jury trial?

(A) Yes, to avoid violating the defendant's right to a speedy trial.

(B) Yes, if both parties agree to a Jury trial.

(C) No, because the attorney's motion was beyond 21 days.

(D) No, because the attorney's motion was beyond 14 days.

Notes

Question 7

Chris was a heroin addict who often committed thefts and resold the stolen items to support his addiction. One afternoon, Chris walked into a home improvement store and he was immediately noticed by the store's loss prevention team. Chris went into the hardware department and placed a drill inside of his jacket before walking towards the exit. Prior to exiting the store, a security guard approached Chris, who immediately ran but dropped the drill in the process. The drill cracked upon making impact with the floor.

If the store sues Chris for conversion will the store succeed?

(A) No, because Chris damaged the drill when it fell to the floor.

(B) Yes, because Chris damaged and concealed the drill with the intent to permanently deprive the store of their inventory.

(C) No, because Chris failed to fully exit the store with the drill, despite his obvious intention.

(D) Yes, based on Chris's dominating actions concerning the drill.

Notes

Question 8

Nico committed suicide and had $72,000 remaining within his estate at the time of his death. Nico owed money to several banks and to local gambling bookies when he died. Nico's former attorney still had a key to Nico's residence. One evening the attorney went into Nico's home and located five suitcases, which all contained cash. The attorney deposited the cash into his own offshore account without notifying Nico's estate. Numerous lenders brought a lawsuit for damages, which exceeded the $72,000 balance in Nico's estate.

If federal law applies, what is the best course of action for Nico's executor to protect Nico's assets?

(A) File a motion which allows multiple plaintiffs to join and enter the lawsuit, with the Court's permission, due to the common question of law or fact which relates to this lawsuit.

(B) File a motion for an interlocutory order which mandates that all interested claimants join the lawsuit by a certain deadline, to prevent an undue hardship on Nico's estate.

(C) Ask the Court to order all interested parties to file a timely motion to intervene.

(D) Immediately file an interpleader which names all interested and/or foreseeable claimants as defendants to the lawsuit.

Notes

Question 9

Veronica sold a hair salon to Katrina. Three months prior to the sale, Veronica learned that Katrina had dated her boyfriend. The sale was allegedly memorialized in a contract at the time of the sale, which included a non-compete clause that prevented either party from opening a salon within 100 miles of one another. Six months after the sale, Veronica's new boyfriend cheated on her with Katrina. Consequently, Veronica opened a hair salon in the same shopping center as Katrina, which prompted Katrina to sue Veronica. The original contract could not be located, but Katrina presented a duplicate hardcopy of the contract. At trial, Veronica objected to the copy of the contract being admitted, by questioning the authenticity of the original executed contract.

Will the Court permit the copy of the contract to be admitted into evidence?

(A) Yes, because duplicate copies are admissible if their metadata can confirm the date that such a duplicate was created.

(B) No, due to the best evidence rule requiring all parties to use original documents and to inform the Court of duplicate copies, which can be used when parties experience difficulty locating the original documents.

(C) Yes, because despite the contract being disputed, the Court will weigh the totality of the circumstances to determine the authenticity of the contested documents.

(D) No, because the legitimacy of the contract is being contested by Veronica.

Notes

Question 10

Tina attended a state operated beauty school for nine months, and she was on track to receive her cosmetology degree with the next graduation class. During her last semester, Tina had a sexual relationship with a teacher and became pregnant by him. The teacher was a married father of four children, but Tina pressured him to pay her $7,000 to prevent her from revealing their relationship. Tina's religion required her to wear six hats during any type of ceremony. Prior to the graduation ceremony, the school learned about Tina's religion and informed her that wearing such attire would not be permitted at the ceremony. Tina perceived this act from the school as retaliation, because it was rumored that she had slept with various teachers. Her lawyer deemed the communication from the school to be a First Amendment violation. Consequently, the lawyer persuaded a court to enter a Temporary Restraining Order against the school, concerning the restriction placed on Tina's attire. Tina participated in the ceremony and celebrated by requiring the same teacher to have sex in his classroom one last time. After the last sexual encounter, Tina never returned to the school and eventually opened a hair salon. The beauty school asked the court to dismiss Tina's lawsuit.

Will the Court agree with the school?

    (A) No, because the reoccurrence of such an act is more than probable.

    (B) Yes, because Tina was allowed to participate in the ceremony, which undermines her standing.

    (C) No, because the right to participate in school functions, which are funded by the state, is a fundamental right.

    (D) Yes, because Tina's claim is debatable and her fundamental rights are not being infringed upon.

Notes

Question 11

Lauren was driving her car one evening and undercover detectives observed her making a drug transaction in a high-crime neighborhood. After the transaction, law enforcement officers continued using surveillance to monitor Lauren, who stopped to purchase gas for her vehicle. Afterwards, Lauren made a right turn to drive down a side street but she did not use her turn signal. Officers stopped Lauren for the traffic violation and asked her to exit the car. When Lauren stepped out of the vehicle, a deputy noticed a clear gallon freezer bag protruding from Lauren's seat, which contained a white substance. A digital scale was also observed in the driver's side door. The officers suspected the white substance to be cocaine or methamphetamine. Lauren was immediately placed under arrest and the entire vehicle was searched, which allowed officers to discover 493 grams of 100% pure methamphetamine, $935 in Lauren's pocketbook, and one assault rifle in the trunk. The rifle was later linked to a recent drive-by shooting, which killed four people, included a two-year-old girl. Lauren faced multiple charges but she instructed her attorney to file a motion to suppress the assault rifle.

What will be the strongest argument to support the admissibility of the rifle?

(A) Officers had probable cause to believe that criminal activity was afoot.

(B) The weapons were discovered incident to a lawful arrest.

(C) Exigent circumstances existed to support the search.

(D) The arresting officers performed an automobile search.

Notes

Question 12

Twelve years ago, Tommy was released from federal prison after serving four years for being convicted of identity theft and social security fraud. Prior to being sentenced, Tommy stashed away thousands of dollars with his sister, Sandra. At the direction of Tommy, Sandra purchased land and opened a cattle ranch. Upon Tommy's release from prison, the two siblings annually generated thousands of dollars from leasing bulls and selling cows. The siblings had owned the farm for eleven years. One of their neighbors also sold livestock and he wanted to develop more of his land. After the neighbor conducted a land survey, he was astonished to learn about the siblings owning a portion of his farm, which consisted of seven acres. The neighbor called some friends to arrange burning a portion of the sibling's land. Before the neighbor and his friends burned the sibling's land, the siblings were secretly informed about the survey and they filed a claim to take ownership of the neighbor's land.

Who will have property ownership of the interested property?

(A) The siblings will prevail because they owned and operated the land open, visibly, and without an objection from the neighbor, for the statutory period.

(B) The neighbor will prevail because the land survey was conducted without the neighbor's consent which substantially affected the use and enjoyment of his property and inhibited his exclusive use of the entire property.

(C) The neighbor will prevail because the siblings did not occupy the land completely.

(D) The siblings will ultimately prevail because they acquired the seven acres by adverse possession.

Notes

Question 13

Tom was a nurse and he also sold counterfeit COVID-19 vaccination cards online. Ironically, Tom was recovering from COVID-19, so he spent most of his time at home while his girlfriend, Sandy, worked as a 911 Call Center Operator. One early afternoon, Sandy arrived home early because she was experiencing Covid-like symptoms. As Sandy arrived home, she attempted to unlock the back door, but she remembered that her key was in her bedroom. Sandy walked to the side door to retrieve a spare key underneath the outside mat. As Sandy approached the side-door she looked the living room window and noticed Tom having sex with a woman in the kitchen. Outraged, Sandy franticly ran towards Tom's car, picked up a large rock and smashed three of his windows, flattened all of his tires, and ran to her car. As Tom's car alarm rang loudly, Tom ran outside and examined his damaged car, but he was suddenly struck by Sandy's car, as she sped away. While Tom laid unconscious on the ground, the woman that he was having sex with inside of the kitchen, dragged him from the middle of the street and onto the sidewalk. In the process of dragging Tom's body, Tom's right leg was awkwardly bent backwards, which tore three of his knee ligaments.

Who will be responsible for Tom's torn knee ligaments?

(A) Sandy because she was the proximate cause of Tom's injuries, which she set into motion when she damaged Tom's car.

(B) Sandy, because the female's attempt to rescue Tom from potential danger was a foreseeable injury.

(C) The female, because dragging Tom was not predictable but was rather negligent, given the seriousness of Tom's injuries.

(D) The female, because exercising negligence during a rescue, by a person who is not medically trained, can enhance a victim's injury.

Notes

Question 14

Steve lived in Washington, D.C. and he was the mastermind of a scheme which involved purchasing new cars from dealerships. This scheme involved using the identities of others to apply for car loans. Michelle worked for Steve and she lived in Washington, D.C., in a property that Steve owned. Steve hired Michelle to date men and use her charm to gain access to their social security numbers. After Michelle became pregnant with her third child, which was fathered by one of the identity theft victims, Steve immediately threatened to evict her.

If Congress passed a law which prohibited landlords from evicting single parents who had two or more children, which of the following is accurate?

(A) This law is being passed for the General Welfare of single mothers.

(B) The Necessary and Proper Clause permits congressional action to ensure the health and safety of single parents is a top priority, based on Congress's spending power.

(C) Such a law would only be enforceable in the District of Columbia.

(D) Congress has the authority to pass such a law, and doing so as applied to all states, will not undermine the Tenth Amendment.

Notes

Question 15

Nance and Kareem were assigned to kill a rival gang leader but the two failed to fully executed the murder. Instead, Kareem stole money from the leader and Nance shot the leader twice in the head, but the victim survived. As a punishment for their joint failure, Nance and Kareem's boss placed one bullet into a pistol and both Nance and Kareem were forced to take turns pointing the gun at each other and pulling the trigger. On Kareem's second turn, he shot Nance in the head, instantly killing him.

What is the most serious crime that Kareem can be charged with?

(A) Felony murder

(B) Murder

(C) Voluntary manslaughter

(D) Assault with a deadly weapon

Notes

Question 16

Wendy was on the run after committing mortgage fraud in another state, which involved her creating a fraudulent business, falsifying loan documents and walking away with $512,000 in profits. After Wendy relocated to state M, with a new identity, she purchased a home with cash and hired a contractor to build a swimming pool with custom-made African marble. While Wendy went on vacation, the contractor called to tell her the swimming pool was complete. However, the contractor informed Wendy that a substitute grade of marble was being used because the vendor who sold the African marble was in prison after being convicted of human trafficking. Wendy was furious and did not want to use the substitute marble. However the builder assured her that the substitute material would be gorgeous. When Wendy returned from vacation she saw the swimming pool and refused to pay the builder, and she threatened to permanently put him out of business if he did not install the African marble.

Has a breach occurred?

(A) No, because the contractor informed Wendy of the expensive substitution, and the substitution no substantial.

(B) Yes, because the contractor materially breached the terms of contract.

(C) No, because the contractor substantially performed, despite the impossibility of the African materials being available.

(D) Yes, because the contactor modified the contract, significantly deviated from the terms of the contract, substituted an unwanted product, and further frustrated the purpose of the contract.

Notes

Question 17

Tyree is a citizen of state Z and he robbed a bank within the state. During the robbery he shot four bank employees. While fleeing from the bank in his car, Tyree collided with another driver. Tyree suddenly exited his car and fired several gunshots at the victim's car, but the victim survived. After being on the run for eleven days, Tyree was captured while hiding in a vacant mobile home, deep in the woods. The accident victim was a citizen of state Q, and he sued Tyree in state Z for $92,000. The victim also filed a suit against Tyree's insurance company, which was incorporated in state M, but its principal place of business was in State Q. Tyree attempted to remove the case to an appropriate U.S. District Court.

Will the Court allow Tyree's request to remove the case?

(A) No, because there is not complete diversity regarding the insurance company.

(B) Yes, because the $90,000 exceeds the required amount in controversy.

(C) No, because Tyree did not properly join the action.

(D) Yes, because the Tyree is not citizen of state F.

Notes

Question 18

Alfred owned 90 acres of land in California and Stacy owned land connected to Alfred's property. Stacy used her land to harvest marijuana, which was purchased by in-state dispensaries. Stacy's deceased grandfather bequeathed the land to her. Originally, Stacy's grandfather used the property to conceal the bodies of men whom he murdered in order to expand the family's business of selling heroin. Stacy paid $1.00 a year to drive across Alfred's land, which consisted of a wide path that was created from various trucks driving across his property.

What is the best description of Stacy's interest in Alfred's land?

    (A) Profit

    (B) Prescriptive easement

    (C) License

    (D) Easement in Gross

Notes

Question 19

A priest was on trial for the possession and production of child pornography. On day five of the trial, the defense attorney for the priest conducted a direct examination, which continued until the late afternoon. After the direct exam, the Judge ordered a recess and instructed the prosecutor to cross-examine the witness on the next day. The prosecutor was very upset that she could not immediately proceed with the cross-examination, but the Judge believed the jury was disinterested, due to the long day. Prior to adjourning for the day, the Judge ordered the defendant not to speak with anyone, due to the high-profile nature of the case.

Was the Judge's decision proper?

(A) No, because the Judge violated the ethical duty that an attorney owes to their client, which includes protecting the client from committing self-incrimination.

(B) No, because the orders from the Judge violated the defendant's Sixth Amendment right to counsel.

(C) Yes, because the Judge was responsible for ensuring that each witness or potential witness would remain eligible to be cross examined, despite the strong media coverage.

(D) Yes, because the Sixth Amendment is not applicable, nor is a critical stage that is triggered by the direct or cross examination.

Notes

Question 20

Frank and Tommy were doctors who shared a medical practice. The two had been in practice together for over fifteen years. Due to a series of events, Tommy believed that Frank was embezzling money from the business. When Tommy had the bank account secretly audited, he discovered that Frank used a significant amount of their profits to purchase various items for his out of state mistress. Tommy recently hired a lawyer.

What should Tommy lawyer's do?

 (A) Ask the Court to appoint a trustee to oversee all bank accounts transactions, which belong to the medical practice.

 (B) Petition the Court for a speedy trial.

 (C) Petition the Court to order a preliminary injunction.

 (D) Petition the Court to order a temporary restraining order.

Notes

Question 21

Bill and Jerry owned a nightclub but a dispute arose concerning the reinvestment of their profits. Jerry accused Bill of stealing and decided to dissolve the partnership. Bill and Jerry lived in different states. Jerry sued Bill for $82,000 for a breach of contract and the case went to trial. During the trial, but while the parties were in the hallway during a court recess, Bill confronted Jerry and accused him of not disclosing all available discovery. Jerry admitted that he intentionally withheld evidence because he did not trust his new legal assistant, but Jerry forgot to handle it personally. Ultimately, Bill lost the trial but he objected in his appeal that certain evidence was deliberately withheld.

Will the Court of Appeals hear Bill's appeal?

(A) No, due to Bill's failure to object during the trial.

(B) Yes, because parties are given a reasonable amount of time to object, which will prevent undue delays.

(C) No, because Jerry did not intentionally withhold discovery from Bill.

(D) Yes, because the Judge had a duty to inquire if the parties had more evidence that needed to be admitted, for full disclosure purposes.

Notes

Question 22

Mary met with Senator Paul for lunch at a lavish restaurant. Mary used money that she generated from her heroine sales to operate a construction equipment rental supply business. Mary's rival, Alphonse, was a black-market gun dealer with deep affiliations to a Mexican cartel. Alphonse enjoyed developing real estate near the city's waterfront district. Mary paid Senator Paul $30,000 to ensure the waterfront district would be rezoned for her benefit. The area in question was comprised of restaurants and retail stores.

What zoning classification would be in the best interest of Mary?

    (A) Commercial

    (B) Mixed-use

    (C) Industrial

    (D) Residential

Notes

Question 23

Kelly was six months pregnant and she was outside painting while her husband was on a ladder cleaning the gutters. Their neighbor, Mandy, was extremely skillful at making counterfeit identification cards, which she primarily sold to illegal immigrants. Overtime, Mandy developed anger towards Kelly's husband because he installed cameras that pointed towards her home. Mandy knew that Kelly suffered from panic attacks. Mandy walked outside and pointed an unloaded shotgun at Kelly's husband, who fell from the ladder upon seeing the gun. As a result of Kelly witnessing Mandy's behavior, Kelly experienced instant contractions and suffered a miscarriage.

Can Kelly succeed if she brings a lawsuit against Mandy?

(A) Yes, due to Mandy's intent, coupled with her reckless behavior.

(B) No, because Kelly's husband was under duress, therefore he should file the lawsuit.

(C) No, because Mandy could not shoot Kelly's husband because the gun was not loaded.

(D) Yes, because it was predictable that Mandy's shocking conduct would cause such distress.

Notes

Question 24

A new state law imposed a tax on any item that was purchased out of state but was used by in-state residents. Tommy operated a very successful pizza parlor, but his business made a profit due to him smuggling guns from out of state, which were later sold to local gun dealers and street gangs. Because the demand for weapons was high, Tommy saved a significant amount of money and purchased a new convection oven, online. Tommy received the oven and within a few hours after the delivery, the oven was in full-use. At the end of the year, Tommy received a tax bill from the state regarding the purchase of the oven. In response, Tommy contested that the tax bill was unconstitutional.

Will the tax bill be considered unconstitutional?

(A) Yes, because the unjustified burden on interstate commerce is unconstitutional.

(B) Yes, because the oven is a good being utilized within the state, and Congress's actions are rationally related to a legitimate governmental interest.

(C) No, because a satisfactory relationship regarding the interstate purchase of the oven and the state is well-grounded.

(D) No, because the Necessary and Proper Clause supports Congress's authority to regulate interstate commerce in this capacity.

Notes

Question 25

A CEO of a professional trading company was federally indicted regarding a multi-million dollar online romance scheme. The federal prosecutor on the case issued a subpoena to the CEO, which requested his personal bank account records. The CEO asked his attorney not to disclose the records. After a substantial delay, the prosecutor filed a motion to compel and a hearing was scheduled for the CEO's attorney to comply with the subpoena.

Will the court likely force the attorney for the CEO to produce the personal bank account records?

(A) No, because the prosecutor could use the records to bring more charges against the defendant, based on self-incrimination.

(B) Yes, because the rules of discovery require all relevant records, which are hearsay exceptions, to be disclosed to opposing parties.

(C) Yes, because violating the attorney-client privilege would not be an issue.

(D) No, because such records would become public records unless the Judge orders that all records are sealed.

Notes

Question 26

Sebastian was a part-time assembler at a large auto manufacturing plant. During the COVID-19 pandemic, Sebastian decided to open a towing company, but he never owned any towing trucks nor hired employees. After submitting fraudulent paperwork that allowed him to receive money through the federal government's Payroll Protection Program, Sebastian received thousands of dollars for his towing business. Sebastian intended to use the money towards upgrading his personal vehicle. Two days later, Sebastian contracted with an auto shop to install an engine inside of his old car, along with a custom-made body kit. The agreement occurred during a telephone conversation and the agreed price was $8,000. Sebastian was required to make four payments, which included $2,000 to install the engine, $2,000 to order the body kit and $4,000 to install the body kit. Sebastian made the first two payments and the auto shop was prepared to install the body kit. However, Sebastian took an unexpected weekend trip with his girlfriend and spent a significant amount of money at a casino. On Monday, Sebastian told the auto shop that he could not make the $4,000 payment, but he still expected the body kit to be installed. After speaking with the auto shop, Sebastian decided to create a medical supply corporation and applied for another PPP loan.

Assuming the statute of frauds is not an issue, if the auto shop refuses to install the body kit, can Sebastian sue and prevail by asserting a breach on the part of the auto shop?

(A) No, because Sebastian's unequivocal repudiation is considered a partial breach, which requires the auto shop to cancel their performance but demand assurances.

(B) Yes, because Sebastian's inability to pay frustrated the purpose of the contract and but he should be given a reasonable time to cure is inability to pay the remaining balance.

(C) No, because the auto shop can refuse to install the body kit and escape contractual liability.

(D) Yes, because Sebastian's inability to pay is not considered a total breach; therefore, the auto shop can suspend their performance, but not cancel their performance of fulfilling the contract.

Notes

Question 27

Wally operated a convenience store and lived in the basement. Wally also allowed his nephew to clean up the store. The nephew's job involved sweeping the aisles and cleaning the windows. Every night, Wally reminded his nephew to place the cleaning supplies inside of the janitor's closet. Wally also used the store to host poker and dice games, and the store was also used to stash stolen guns for a local criminal organization. One night, a man broke into the store and went directly to the cash register. Wally heard the noise, grabbed his gun, and ran upstairs. The thief saw Wally and immediately fired a weapon towards Wally's direction. Wally ducked and returned fire with his revolver. As Wally ran to reposition himself, he tripped over a broom and hit his head against the cement floor. The thief ran towards the exit but Walley fired his weapon and struck the thief in the leg. As Wally became disoriented from his fall, the thief escaped. Thirty minutes later, the thief walked into a hospital to receive treatment for his gunshot wound, but he was arrested after receiving medical treatment. After being in a coma for three days, Wally died in a hospital from severe brain damage.

What crime can the thief be convicted of?

(A) Involuntary Manslaughter

(B) No Crime

(C) Strong Arm Robbery

(D) Felony Murder

Notes

Question 28

Jake wanted to obtain a loan from his bank to invest into various stocks. During the online loan application process, the bank inquired about Jake's ethnicity because he failed to complete that section of the application. Jake corrected his application by selecting his race, and within a few hours the loan application was denied. Jake sued the bank for racial discrimination and the lawsuit went to trial. At the conclusion of both parties presenting their case, the jury deliberated for two days. A general verdict was returned in favor of the bank. The Judge polled the jury and two of the jurors admitted to deciding in Jake's favor, and it was rumored that the bank's attorney offered $5,000 to any juror who decided against Jake. Prior to accepting the case, the bank's attorney announced that he was running to become the District Attorney in the upcoming election.

What should the Judge do?

(A) Enter an order in favor of Jake, with prejudice.

(B) Require the jury to continue deliberating or enter an Order for a new trial.

(C) Dismiss the tainted jurors and require both parties to re-argue closing arguments.

(D) Enter a judgment in favor of the bank.

Notes

Question 29

Sierra loaned Tommy money to purchase a home. Three years later, Tommy obtained a loan from Fred, a loan shark, to purchase an irrigation system. Tommy would use the irrigation system to help maintain his in-home illegal marijuana business, but two months later, he was robbed at gunpoint. Tommy was unable to make payments on either loan. Tommy's wife suspected that Fred coordinated the robbery to ensure a default on his extended loan. Ultimately, Tommy's home was sold at a foreclosure sale and the money from the sale was enough to repay Sierra's loan. Yet, Fred challenged the sale and believed the foreclosure sale extinguished Sierra's interest.

What can Fred use as his strongest argument to contest that his interest was not extinguished?

(A) Notice of the foreclosure was not provided to all interested parties.

(B) Fred did not receive a notice regarding the foreclosure sale.

(C) The foreclosure sale was not arranged in enough time to allow Fred to learn of the sale.

(D) Sierra was recently convicted of tax fraud, therefore, lost her priority as a creditor over Fred.

Notes

Question 30

Miles was standing at a bar inside of a nightclub while talking with the bartender. Unexpectedly, Miles's former girlfriend Lenoire, walked into the building. Lenoire made eye contact with Miles and rolled her eyes as she walked towards his direction. Lenoire's new boyfriend was following her and he also made eye contact with Miles. Miles retrieved money from his pocket to pay for his drink. While finishing his drink, Miles looked around and saw Lenoire and her boyfriend passionately kissing in the back of the club. Suddenly, Lenoire's boyfriend made eye contact with Miles, while simultaneously kissing Lenoire. As Miles walked away from the bar, he and Lenoire's boyfriend were still staring at one another, and the boyfriend suddenly displayed a gang sign. Miles suddenly removed a firearm from underneath his jacket and fired several bullets towards Lenoire's boyfriend. Three bullets struck the boyfriend, but one bullet hit Lenoire in the leg. Upset at her boyfriend for taunting Miles, Lenoire brings an action against her boyfriend to recover from her sustained injuries.

Will Lenoire prevail?

(A) Yes, because any reasonable person could foresee that jealousy in such a situation might cause a person to react in a violent manner.

(B) No, because it will be difficult to prove that her boyfriend was a proximate cause of Lenoire's injury especially since the boyfriend did not fire the weapon.

(C) Yes, because the chains of events were set into motion by the immature actions of Lenoire's boyfriend, therefore making him the proximate cause of her injuries.

(D) No, because the boyfriend did not tease Miles with the intent that a firearm would be used to shoot someone.

Notes

Question 31

Larry was indicted on multiple counts of wire fraud and filing false tax returns. Due to a complex Ponzi scheme, Larry defrauded over $9 million dollars from multiple victims. The case went to trial. While the jury was on their second day of deliberation, Larry was being held at a local detention center. Nevertheless, Larry sent a message to a street associate, who offered certain jurors $10,000 if they find Larry not guilty. Some jurors agreed to the deal, but one juror contacted the Judge's chambers about the offer.

What crimes can Larry be charged with?

(A) Conspiracy to commit Jury Tampering

(B) No Crime

(C) Jury Intimidation

(D) Conspiracy to commit Jury Tampering and Jury Tampering

Notes

Question 32

A small town in a very rural part of the state had been government-controlled by a family of farmers for decades. Such deep ties to agriculture ensured that Latinos from neighboring countries would be allowed to enter the state to help local farmers. Deep political connections also ensured that the finest marijuana would be imported by migrants, farmed by local farmers, sold in local dispensaries and ultimately taxed by the town. Certain farming contracts were being given only to Latinos over other races. During an election, the town's only voting precinct had been open since 6:30 a.m. The mayor's seat was on the ballot and the town had been plagued by several police shootings, which claimed the lives of unarmed black men. Despite released body worn camera footage, which reflected each victim not being a threat to the arresting officers, each investigation cleared the officers from facing criminal charges. At 4:55 p.m., a church van filled with black voters arrived at the voting poll. Upon the van of passengers exiting the van, a voting poll employee told the passengers that no minorities were allowed to vote until white voters had a chance to vote. The poll closed at 8:00 p.m. Such treatment towards the black citizens sparked an immediate outrage. Police officers were immediately dispatched to the precinct and various television reporters arrived to provide news coverage about the incident.

Which Amendment was being violated?

(A) Thirteenth

(B) Ninth

(C) Eighth

(D) Fifteenth

Notes

Question 33

Billy's motion for compassionate release was granted after he served 8 years in federal prison for a drug case, which involved the Racketeer Influenced and Corrupt Organization Act. Upon being released, Billy temporarily lived with his sister and her husband. One day Billy arrived home early from work and he walked into the bathroom. Upon entering the bathroom, Billy discovered his brother-in-law snorting cocaine while taking a bath. An argument occurred and the brother-in-law begged Billy not to tell his sister about the drug use. Billy agreed but told the brother-in-law that he would have to repay the favor. Two months later, Billy's car was in the repair shop and the bill to repair the car was $1,800. Billy asked the mechanic if another vehicle in good condition would be accepted as a substitute for the $1,800 balance. The mechanic replied "Yes, as long as the title is clean."

Billy created a written contract with all of the appropriate terms in the presence of the mechanic, and both of them signed the document. Billy immediately called the brother-in-law, who owned a used car dealership. Billy asked the brother-in-law to bring him a car under $3,000, in good condition and with a clean title. The brother initially refused, but Billy reminded him about the agreement that was discussed in the bathroom. Two days later, Billy delivered a 2009 pick-up truck to the mechanic, which contained a clean title and it was in good condition. The mechanic told Billy that he would not accept the truck because the tire rims were out of style. Billy sued the mechanic to enforce their written agreement.

How will the Court rule concerning the parties agreement?

(A) The parties agreement and actions were sufficient despite the breach.

(B) The parties agreement will be honored by the Court because Billy substantially performed by delivering adequate consideration.

(C) The parties agreement and actions were insufficient due to pre-existing obligations.

(D) The Court will not honor the oral contract because the value of the vehicle was over $500.

Notes

Question 34

The construction manager who coordinated the hiring and firing of employees, hired five contractors to work for one year. Every Friday night the manager and contractors played dice games at a local bar. During a routine Friday night game, one of the contractors cheated the manager out of $400. On Monday morning, the manager ordered all contractors to attend an emergency meeting, which resulted in the firing of the contractor who cheated the manager in the dice game. The contractor who was fired filed a lawsuit against the company. On direct exam, the contractor listed some of the attendees at the meeting, but could not describe everyone accurately. The contractor's attorney offered to show the contractor an email that the contractor previously sent to the company's human resources department, which listed all of the names of the attendees at the meeting.

What is the best course of action by the attorney?

(A) Leading the witness in this fashion would be improper.

(B) It is improper to show the witness the notes because it would undermine his personal knowledge.

(C) Refreshing the witness's memory would be proper in this manner.

(D) Refreshing the witness's memory would not be proper in this manner.

Notes

Question 35

Earlier this year, Dexter set his girlfriend's apartment on fire after he caught her cheating with the building's security guard. The security guard also owed Dexter $1,500 from a prior loan. Prior to the fire, Dexter's girlfriend threatened to tell the police that he was stealing credit cards from mailboxes, which he used to commit identity theft. Prior to the fire, the county recently hired Freddy as a part-time employee. Part-time employees were entitled to full medical benefits. The medical policy stated part-time and full-time employees who were injured from a job-related injury would be entitled to receive 100% of medical coverage under the policy. The policy also stated that all employees who refused to accept all or partial amendments to the insurance policy would forfeit all benefits within the policy.

Last week Freddy died after falling from a ladder, which was used to extinguish the fire that was ignited by Dexter. On the way to the hospital, Freddy told paramedics not to take him to Hospital Y because it was against his religious beliefs. Hospital Y was the closest hospital in the area. The county's medical insurance policy was amended a month prior to the fire, and the amendment required all employees to receive medical treatment at the nearest hospital. Consequently, Freddy's estate filed an action which asserted their entitlement to Freddy's policy by requesting a full payout of all benefits. The estate threatened to bring an action if their request was denied because such a denial would violate Freddy's Constitutional rights.

Will the argument of Freddy's estate prevail?

(A) Yes, because a person's religious belief is a fundamental fabric of the Free Exercise Clause, which cannot be discriminated against, nor ignored.

(B) No, because the constitutional denial of benefits in this situation was absent of imposed penalties against Freddy by his choice of refusing to be treated at the nearest hospital.

(C) Yes, because the estate had a vested right to receive death benefits due to Freddy's job-related injury, which was initiated by Freddy agreeing to be contractually benefited in the event of job-related injury or death.

(D) No, because denying benefits to the estate was impartial.

Notes

Question 36

Over the last three years, Debra made a living from creating online romance schemes, which involved persuading men to wire her money to support her "non-profit organization" for disabled children. Paranoid that many of her former online boyfriends would hire someone to murder her in retaliation, Debra underwent expensive cosmetic surgery in state M. Surprisingly, the outcome of the surgery was not a success, so Debra sued the doctor, who was a resident of state O. Debra sued the doctor in federal court for $76,000. To serve the doctor with notice of the lawsuit, Debra hired a private detective who discovered the doctor had an upcoming child support hearing in state M. While leaving the courthouse in state M, after the child support hearing, Debra's private investigator served the doctor in the parking lot of the courthouse.

Will State M have personal jurisdiction over the doctor in this case?

    (A) No, but only if exercising jurisdiction over the doctor would not offend traditional notions of fair play and substantial justice.

    (B) Yes, based on the continuous contacts with the forum state, due to the family law proceedings alone.

    (C) No, because the state lacked personal jurisdiction.

    (D) Yes, despite using extreme measures by hiring a detective, the doctor's presence within the state permitted state M to properly exercise personal jurisdiction.

Notes

Question 37

Mandy went to a bar to relax after work. After an hour of socializing and consuming a few drinks, Mandy noticed that her boyfriend was in the bar and he was kissing another woman. Mandy approached the woman, smacked her several times, spat in her face and walked outside. Mandy's boyfriend followed her outside to apologize, but she punched him before being separated by other bar patrons. The owner of the bar called the police to report the incident, but Mandy had already left the scene. Later that night, after the bar was closed and all employees had exited the building, the bar was set on fire. Several months later, Mandy was charged with arson. The case went to trial. Mandy married her new boyfriend. During the trial, the government called Mandy's husband to testify. Mandy's lawyer objected to the husband testifying.

Should the Court allow Mandy's husband to testify?

(A) Sustain the objection because Mandy can prevent her husband from testifying against her.

(B) Sustain the objection because confidential communications during the course of a marriage are protected under the husband-wife privilege.

(C) Overrule the objection because the husband can refuse to testify against Mandy.

(D) Overrule the objection because the husband cannot be compelled to testify against Mandy.

Notes

Question 38

Detectives received a confidential tip that three men used fraudulent identities to create counterfeit checks, which were used to deposit and withdraw money from multiple banks. Consequently, federal agents and local detectives conducted surveillance around certain banks and a specific office building, which was believed to be the headquarters of the check-fraud operation. After five months of surveillance, agents and detectives obtained arrest and search warrants to apprehend the suspects. One night, all three men were observed leaving the office building and two females were seen leaving with the men. Each female was carrying a pink book bag. After arresting all five people, detectives searched through the pink book bags. Upon searching the bags that were worn by one of the females, a detective discovered hundreds of social security cards, driver's licenses, and several small clear bags, which contained over 50 debit cards. The female was charged and the case was set for trial. The female filed a motion to suppress the contents of her bag from being admitted into evidence.

Will the Judge deny the woman's motion?

(A) Yes, because the veracity and tip in this situation must be corroborated to support officers subsequently obtaining a search warrant, which officers failed to perform.

(B) No, because believing the female was involved in the commission of a crime was not probable enough to support her belongings being examined.

(C) Yes, because the female lacks standing, because all targets who were observed leaving the building had their belongings searched.

(D) No, because detectives failed to describe the place and person to be searched, which was not articulated in an affidavit for a Judge to approve, prior to the arrest and subsequent search.

Notes

Question 39

John had a history of jury tampering. John was also previously convicted of selling narcotics and committing passport fraud. As a result of the fire, John was facing an upcoming trial for arson. The restaurant that John was accused of burning down was located on the city's west side. During jury selection, John told his lawyer to use all available peremptory strikes against anyone who resided in the west side of the city.

Will John's attorney be allowed to strike potential jurors based on John's request?

    (A) Yes, but only if the west side of the city is not substantially segregated, because a preemptory strike based on such demographics would be racially motivated.

    (B) No, because exercising a preemptory strike, at the direction of a client, can create Constitutional violations.

    (C) Yes, and no explanation by John's attorney is required.

    (D) Yes, and John's attorney must explain to the Court the rationale behind the strike, to prevent Constitutional violations concerning the defendant's rights.

Notes

Question 40

Luis was involved in a bar fight and badly assaulted a victim with a knife. Luis was born in El Salvador and he was a hard-working husband and father of four children. After being convicted of assault with a deadly weapon, he faced a deportation hearing. Luis believed officers unlawfully searched his vehicle, which led to the knife being discovered. When Luis attended the deportation hearing, his lawyer made a timely motion to suppress the discovery of the knife.

How will Judge rule?

(A) Deny the motion.

(B) Grant the motion based on a Constitutional violation.

(C) Grant the motion in part, until the sentencing has occurred.

(D) Deny the motion because the legality of the search was not addressed during the preliminary hearing.

Notes

Question 41

At 2:30 a.m. on a cold December night, Snow was ordered to execute a hit on a man who owed Snow's boss $14,000. As the man placed groceries inside of his car, Snow strangled the man to death then tossed the victim's body inside of Snow's trunk. After which, Snow fled the scene by driving through the grocery store's parking lot. While fleeing the scene, Snow drove over a patch of black ice and hit a woman who was returning a shopping cart to the store. At trial, the woman's husband testified that he was waiting inside their car and witnessed Snow driving over 45 miles an hour.

Will the testimony of the husband be admissible?

(A) No, because the witness is unqualified to testify concerning the speed of a car, absent qualifying credentials.

(B) Yes, due to the witness's understanding of what occurred.

(C) No, because hearsay would prevent the admission of the witness's statement.

(D) Yes, because the existing state of mind of the husband would allow his statements to be admitted.

Notes

Question 42

Randy spent his entire adult life selling heroin and cocaine. However, Randy's son decided to sell marijuana State P legalized marijuana, and Randy's son moved to state P to open a marijuana dispensary. Recently Congress passed a law that required law enforcement officials to seize any vehicle that was used to transpo illegal drugs. Moreover, seized drugs and money would be turned over to federal authorities through th forfeiture process. When an officer stopped Randy's son for speeding, a K-9 officer detected marijuan inside of the vehicle. Upon conducting a search of the trunk, officers discovered and charged Randy's so with possessing an illegal amount of marijuana, which was 18 pounds.

Will the marijuana recovered at the traffic stop be controlled by Congressional authority?

(A) Yes, because the interstate highways are regulated by Congress, through the Commerce Clause

(B) No, because criminalizing marijuana violates the 10th Amendment, which provides fundamenta state sovereignty and protection against the Necessary and Proper Clause.

(C) Yes, because the rational function of the Commerce Clause, along with the Supremacy Clause gives Congress the power to use the 10th Amendment to criminalize the transportation c marijuana.

(D) No, because the 10th Amendment prohibits Congress from seizing control over loca governmental procedures.

Notes

Question 43

Kevin was the owner of a strip club and several hotels. It was rumored that Kevin kidnapped young women from foreign countries and forced them to become sex workers at his strip club. To increase sales, Kevin hired a printing company to advertise his club by designing flyers, which would be distributed throughout the city. Five days after receiving the flyers, Kevin noticed the name of his club was incorrectly spelled. Kevin threatened to physically harm the owner of the printing company if the spelling error was not immediately corrected. Three days later the printing company sent Kevin a bill for $475.00.

Will Kevin be required to pay for the printing services?

(A) Yes, because the merchant confirmation rule prevents Kevin from rejecting the goods.

(B) Yes, due to Kevin accepting the flyers.

(C) No, because the seller had a duty to inspect the goods and ensure that the flyers were fit for their ordinary use.

(D) No, because under the UCC Article 1, the essence of the perfect tender rule will prevent a party from accepting goods which are unreasonably or unsatisfactorily delivered.

Notes

Question 44

Three months ago, a teenage boy ran away from home after feeling violated, due to his parents discovering ten bags of pills, $450 and seven brand new expensive purses in his room. After sleeping on the street for two nights, one late night when the temperature dropped to 25 degrees, the teenager walked to a large building that was closed. The teenager climbed through a cracked window and decided to sleep inside for the night. An hour later, the teenager was awakened as he was being hit with a metal pole by a security guard. The teenager jumped to his feet and noticed another metal pole laying against the wall. The teenager grabbed the pole and began swinging it towards the security guard, which ultimately struck the guard in the head. As the guard fell to the floor while grabbing his head, the teenager dropped the pole and watched the guard groan in pain. This entire incident was recorded on the building's 24-hour surveillance system.

What is the most serious charge that can be brought against the teenager?

(A) Assault

(B) Trespass

(C) Burglary

(D) Assault with a deadly weapon

Notes

Question 45

Fatima was a well-established jewelry thief who smashed and grabbed items from store display cases. She was also very skilled at manipulating men by persuading them to purchase her extravagant diamonds, which she resold in the diamond district of her city. A new scheme that Fatima discovered involved selling jewelry at auctions. Last week, Fatima placed a few diamond bracelets on sale at a very exclusive auction house. Fatima did not specify any selling price for the jewelry. Consequently, an auctioneer won the bid for one of Fatima's favorite bracelets. Outraged because of the low price, Fatima lost interest in the auction and stood up to declare that all of her jewelry in the auction was being "withdrawn unless it was sold at ten times higher than the starting auction price."

Will the sale of Fatima's item be enforced by the highest bidder?

(A) Yes, because the auctioneer's offer was accepted due to the bidder's highest bid.

(B) No, because the non-existence of a reserve was unknown and therefore could not be satisfied.

(C) Yes, because the auctioneer accepted the bidder's offer.

(D) No, because Fatima's displeasure with the potential winning bid and stoppage of the auction terminated the sale.

Notes

Question 46

Bill owned a mechanic shop and also operated a dog fighting club in the basement of his business. Next to the lobby door, which separated the repair area from the lobby, was a posted sign which read, "Customers are not allowed beyond this point." One morning a customer named Hilary entered the shop for a scheduled oil change, but after no one greeted her in the lobby, she waited for five minutes, before walking throughout the shop to locate an employee. Unfortunately, Bill was downstairs feeding his dogs, and the front desk clerk was in the restroom. As Hilary walked down the stairs, which led to the basement, she slipped and broke her hip.

Will Bill likely be liable for Hilary's injury?

(A) No, because Hilary disregarded the boundaries of the restricted area.

(B) Yes, because Bill owed a non-delegable duty to invitees.

(C) No, because Hilary's disregard for the restricted area canceled Bill's duty to use reasonable care as the owner of the property.

(D) Yes, because Bill failed to make a reasonable inspection of his property, which was a duty that he owed to a licensee.

Notes

Question 47

Sammy was a well-established car dealer who decided to run for mayor. Weeks before the election, an article was published in the local newspaper, which accused Sammy of stealing supplies from the car lots of rival car dealers. Unfortunately, Sammy lost the election by one point and he sued the newspaper for defamation. At trial, Sammy cried while testifying that he suffered emotional distress and severe impairment to his reputation. The attorney for the newspaper called one of Sammy's former employees to testify. The employee testified that via text messages, Sammy ordered all new employees to steal auto parts from rival dealerships on Christmas morning. Sammy's attorney timely objected to the admissibility of the former employee's testimony.

Will the Court allow the testimony of the employee to be admitted?

    (A) No, because the testimony is irrelevant to Sammy's character.

    (B) Yes, because the testimony is relevant to Sammy's character.

    (C) No, because such biased testimony substantially outweighs the probative value of the testimonial evidence.

    (D) Yes, because the testimony is an essential element of the crime, it is reliable and can be verified with cell phone carrier business records.

Notes

Question 48

Hosea was charged with involuntary manslaughter but he was initially charged with a DUI, which resulted from a head-on collision with another driver. The other driver died from their injuries. When the case went to trial, the jury found Hosea not guilty because the other driver was under the influence of cocaine and Vicodin, based upon the autopsy report. Also, traffic cameras reflected the victim crossing over the center line. The victim and Hosea were business partners. The victim's estate sued Hosea for fraud by alleging that Hosea misled the victim into agreeing to receive $35,000 from a Paycheck Protection Program loan. Hosea filed a timely answer and raised collateral estoppel as his defense.

Can Hosea's attorney use collateral estoppel as an effective defense?

(A) Yes, because the estate was aware of the criminal case but failed to timely file an action with the Court.

(B) Yes, because protecting the defendant from an interested party who was not a party of a previous related proceeding would unfairly expose the defendant to multiple litigations.

(C) No, because criminal proceedings have a different standard than civil proceedings, therefore collateral estoppel would not place prohibitions on the estate from moving forward with their case.

(D) No, based on the victim's estate being absent from the criminal case.

Notes

Question 49

Zigggywarwashwall-Limepeacepower was a factory which generated millions of dollars from manufacturing assault weapon accessories, telescopes and night-vision goggles. Earlier this year, the United States was engaged in a tense dispute concerning imposed tariffs on another country. Many experts believed the two countries would be at war very soon. Hourly-paid employees at the factory were disgusted with their low-paying wages, and the labor union leader encouraged all union employees to go on a strike. One day three masked men assaulted the union leader at his home. The entire assault was captured on the union leader's home surveillance system. The men threatened to make a second visit if the union leader did not stop encouraging employees to go on a strike. Two months later, as tensions increased between the U.S. and the foreign country, Congress passed a law that prohibited strikes regarding all companies which directly or indirectly supplied the government with military hardware. Soon after Congress passed the new law prohibiting strikes, the union leader called for a strike, and the employees immediately stopped working. One day after the strike began, the union leader was seen leaving a restaurant, while sitting in the back seat of a car, which was occupied by four other men. No one has seen or heard from the union leader since that time.

Is the federal law Constitutional concerning the prohibition of the strike?

(A) Yes, because such legislation is supported by the war power.

(B) No, because peace time will not allow Congress to exercise war power without violating the Privilege and Immunities Clause.

(C) Yes, because national security, war power, and Congressional authority authorize the federal government to regulate public and private entities, even during peace time.

(D) No, because anti-strike measures exercised by Congress are without merit during peace time if alternative measures are available.

Notes

Question 50

Jarod was leaving his girlfriend's apartment at 7:00 a.m. in a neighborhood known to have massive drug activity. Two days prior, in the same neighborhood, three officers approached a black man who was walking to the store, chased him, and shot him three times in the back. Yet, no weapons were recovered on the victim's person. The building that Jarod was seen leaving was the home of a suspected drug kingpin, who was under surveillance by the FBI. Federal agents saw Jarod exit the building and observed him approaching a parked luxury car. Suddenly, four undercover agents approached Jarod and asked him to stop walking. Jarod immediately ran and pulled two bags of cocaine from his pocket, which he swallowed. Jarod also removed a 9mm firearm from his pocket and tossed it into three large bushes, while running away. The agents eventually tackled Jarod, placed him under arrest, canvassed the area and recovered the discarded gun. Unfortunately, the digested cocaine caused Jarod to overdose, but the agents quickly saved Jarod's life by giving him Narcan. Jarod regained full consciousness but found himself handcuffed to a hospital bed. Jarod was charged with the possession of narcotics, the intent to distribute, and the possession of a deadly weapon. Prior to trial, Jarod's attorney filed a motion to suppress the firearm.

Will Jarod's motion to suppress succeed?

(A) Yes, because a possible seizure based on Jarod's location, race and actions would not create reasonable suspicion.

(B) No, because Jarod relinquished his rights when tossing the firearm.

(C) Yes, because based on the totality of the circumstances, officers lacked reasonable suspicion and probable cause to compel Jarod to run in fear of his life.

(D) No, because reasonable suspicion allowed officers to take any measures that are necessary to confirm their suspicions, based on exigent circumstances.

Notes

Question 51

Carlos was a general contractor who was hired by John to build a bowling alley and several other commercial properties. Prior to becoming a contractor, Carlos spent 11 years in prison after being convicted of armed robbery. John and Carlos signed a contract and John agreed to pay Carlos $70,000 a year. Unfortunately, John had a very bad gambling habit and now owed a bookie $18,000. Out of desperation, John asked Carlos to rob a bank and Carlos would be allowed to keep 10% of the robbery money. Without hesitation, Carlos rejected the offer but he was immediately fired by John. In an effort to feed his family, Carlos devoted a lot of time searching for new employment without success. Carlos did find a data-entry position that would have paid him $35,000 however, the employer implemented a hiring freeze, due to the COVID-19 pandemic. One month later, John was found discovered lying face down in a pool of blood at a construction site. John never walked again.

Can Carlos bring an action against John and recover any damages as a result?

(A) Yes, because Carlos can recover the $40,000, which was the contract price.

(B) Yes, but Carlos's damages will be reduced by the $2,000 that he could have mitigated if he had accepted the part-time position.

(C) Yes, because John failed to live up to his bargain of the exchange by acting in bad faith.

(D) No, because doing so would provide Carlos with unjust enrichment based, despite John's bad judgment.

Notes

Question 52

A local police department posted reward bulletins to capture a man who robbed a card game and killed three men during the robbery. While shopping at the grocery store one evening, a detective who was assigned to the robbery case, saw a former classmate in the store. This classmate was known to attend many card games in the neighborhood. After a brief conversation, the classmate agreed to assist with the investigation by informing the detective of any circulating news in the neighborhood. However, the classmate conditionally agreed to assist with the case if the detective agreed to stop investigating the classmate's nephew regarding a drug case. The detective reluctantly agreed. One month later after leaving a church service, the classmate drove to the detective's office. Upon meeting with the detective and making small talk, the classmate confessed to planning and executing the robbery. Upon learning about this new information, the detective issued Miranda warnings to the classmate.

Can the statements about planning and executing the robbery be admitted into evidence?

   (A) No, because the classmate's freedom was not deprived when the confession was made.

   (B) Yes, because the detective should have given Miranda warnings to the classmate and required the classmate to repeat the confession because the classmate placed himself in custody from the confession.

   (C) Yes, because the classmate reluctantly and involuntarily confessed to the crime.

   (D) No because the classmate waived his Miranda rights by driving to the police station to confess.

Notes

Question 53

Bernie served 14 years in federal prison for being the mastermind behind a large fraudulent cryptocurrency online exchange. Bernie's son Charles, was arrested for possessing drugs and he was a third-time offender. During sentencing, the Judge gave Charles the option of enlisting into the military or serve four years in federal prison. Charles decided to serve his country and he was stationed in State C. Country X decided to invade its neighboring Country O. The President of the United States issued sanctions against Country X, and NATO accused Country X of violating International Law. In response, Country X decided to fire missiles at the United States and launched a cyber-attack on various financial markets within the United States. Infuriated, the President of the United States declared war on Country X and deployed 200,000 troops to Country X. Consequently, Congress opposed the President's actions and Charles waited for military orders concerning a possible deployment.

Are the actions of the President permitted?

(A) Yes, because the President is the Commander in Chief, and the Constitution empowers a President to declare war when the national security of the United States has been threatened.

(B) No, because such actions by the President constitute a separation of power contravention, which undermines the President's authority as Chief Executive.

(C) Yes, because deploying troops overseas is directly correlated to International Affairs.

(D) No, because the President's declaration is not permitted.

Notes

Question 54

Maria was a teenager who lived with her older sister. One day Maria was outside doing her nails on the front porch. Her neighbor, Marshall walked a dog on the sidewalk, which passed Maria's home. Marshall had stolen the dog while committing a burglary. Maria complimented the appearance of the dog and Marshall offered to sell the dog to her for $950.00. Maria spat on the ground, and said, "No fucking way," before going back inside of her home. Thirty minutes later, when Marshall was walking the dog to a nearby park, Maria ran outside and caught up with Marshall to ask if she could purchase the dog for $950.00. Marshall said no and continued walking.

Is there a contract between Maria and Marshall?

    (A) No, because Maria is under 18 years old.

    (B) No, because Maria discarded Marshall's offer.

    (C) Yes, because Maria's acceptance of Marshall's original offer was within a reasonable time.

    (D) Yes, but only if Maria memorialized their agreement into a signed writing.

Notes

Question 55

At the conclusion of a three-day conference for pharmaceutical consultants, Phil and Lisa enjoyed their time together by drinking and dancing at a night club. Afterwards, they both went to Lisa's hotel room and took turns snorting several grams of cocaine. Later that night, Lisa was seen on the hotel's surveillance system leaving the room. Months later, Lisa was indicted on murdering Phil. The arrest affidavit stated that Lisa had sex with the victim, stole personal items from his pants, then stabbed him to death as he slept. At the end of the murder trial, the Judge instructed the jury that Lisa had the burden of proving by a preponderance of the evidence, that she acted in self-defense. Lisa's defense was hinged on her being overpowered by a man that she barely knew, who attempted to rape her. Upon hearing the jury instruction, Lisa's attorney timely objected to the Judge's instruction and claimed the prosecutor was required to prove all charges beyond a reasonable doubt.

Does Lisa have a strong argument?

(A) No, because self-defense must be proven by a defendant who uses the Due Process Clause to assert an affirmative defense, based on the totality of the evidence.

(B) No, because when a defendant has declared self-defense, that defendant will be mandated to prove such a defense by a preponderance of the evidence.

(C) Yes, because the Due Process Clause prohibits the government from placing an unfair burden on a defendant regarding self-defense, when the government has failed to meet its burden by proving guilt beyond a reasonable doubt.

(D) Yes, because self-defense does not have to be proven by a preponderance of the evidence.

Notes

Question 56

Lester was a black belt and former boxer who recently joined organization X. Organization X encouraged the use of weaponized self-defense to protect citizens from police brutality. Organization X was also under investigation for assisting veterans with fraudulently applying for VA medical benefits. The organization received a kick back percentage of the monthly payments from the approved benefits. If a veteran's application was approved but he or she refused to make monthly kick back payments to the organization, Lester would visit the veteran to enforce the payment. Every Friday, Lester also circulated leaflets throughout the city regarding the growth of police brutality. Last year, members of Organization X were involved in a shooting with police officers. Specifically, members from Organization X began firing at three officers who were having lunch, and all three officers were severely wounded. The three officers were previously involved in the unexplained death of an unarmed Hispanic teenager. The teenager was arrested but died from brain damage, which he suffered while being transported to the police station in a police wagon. Recently, Lester was arrested and charged with being a member of this "radical militant organization."

What is the government's strongest argument to prove Lester's Constitutional rights were not violated?

(A) Lester was expected to intimidate and harm individuals, which is a form of domestic terrorism.

(B) This organization was not formed with the intent to engage in peaceful demonstrations, which is not protected by the Constitution.

(C) Lester's initial connection with this organization was motivated by an intent to commit unlawfulness.

(D) Lester substantially assisted the organization in the furtherance of committing illegal activities, such as attacking law enforcement personnel.

Notes

Question 57

Phillip was a successful hotelier and he owned a roofing company. Phillip was recently indicted on nine counts of credit card fraud and bankruptcy fraud. However, because Phillip understood that he would be spending some time in prison, he devoted himself to making a significant amount of money in a short period of time. To get ready for a big commercial roofing job, Phillip executed a contract with a wholesaler regarding special grade roofing materials. The following week, Phillip called the wholesaler and requested to receive nine buckets of roofing joint compound. The wholesaler sent a letter to Phillip, which included an invoice amount of $7,000, for the nine buckets. After receiving the letter, Phillip agreed by signing the seller's contract, but inserted language that reflected "$7,000 for thirteen buckets." Phillip mailed the letter to the seller that afternoon. Twelve days later, Phillip called the seller and inquired about the status of the materials. The seller refused to send any materials because the contract was incorrect. Phillip was furious because he was fast approaching a motions hearing regarding his fraud case.

Does a contract exist?

(A) Yes, because Phillip accepted the offer from the wholesaler, with additional terms, and the wholesaler did not protest within 7 business days.

(B) No, because there was a mistake of fact, which did not result in a meeting of the minds.

(C) No, but only if the protester can prove that Phillip understood 13 buckets would substantially cost more than $7,000.

(D) Yes, because Phillip accepted the offer from the wholesaler, with additional terms, and the wholesaler did not object within 10 business days.

Notes

Question 58

Salma operated a federally funded non-profit organization which provided single mothers with cellular phones and groceries. Edward was an administrator for the non-profit organization, and he was responsible for maintaining the inventory of all cellular phones. Other employees reported seeing Edward load multiple boxes of cellular phones into his personal book bag. Edward was also suspected of selling the phones online. Hence, Edward was eventually fired and charged with embezzlement. At trial, the government called a witness named Hank, who testified that he observed Edward take cellular phones on multiple occasions. On cross-examination, it was revealed that Edward's girlfriend ended their relationship and was soon impregnated by Hank.

Is the cross examination of Hank admissible?

(A) No, because doing so would undermine a witness's willingness to participate in the administration of justice.

(B) No, because a personal relationship between a witness and a party to a case, does not establish a foundation which permits subjecting the testifying witness to impeachment.

(C) Yes, because Hank's personal knowledge concerning the essential issue of the case, contains value and relevant credibility.

(D) Yes, because Hank lacks impartiality.

Notes

Question 59

A wealthy entertainment mogul was strangely shot to death, at a cemetery while visiting his wife's grave. After the sudden murder, Thomas, a long-time employee at the entertainment company, was promoted to CEO, and he was also the son of a ruthless hitman named "Knuckles." Over the years, Thomas became a wealthy real estate investor who owned multiple properties in the city's business district, and he leased one of his buildings to a veterinarian, for a leasing period of three years. Six months into the lease, the veterinarian vacated the lease and assigned it to an accountant. The accountant properly vacated the lease after seven months. Thomas then immediately leased the building to a lawyer, but the lawyer and Thomas had an argument about the lawyer's willingness to represent Thomas's son in a domestic violence case. After the argument, the lawyer stopped paying rent and moved out of the building. Thomas decided to sue the veterinarian.

Will Thomas prevail in the lawsuit?

(A) No, because the accountant as the initial assignee, assumed the lease in good faith.

(B) Yes, because the veterinarian's obligation survived any and all assignments.

(C) No, because the accountant as the initial assignee, assumed the lease in good faith but notified Thomas of his intent to vacate the property.

(D) Yes, because Thomas immediately mitigated his damages by renting the building to the lawyer.

Notes

Question 60

Deion owned a very successful gentlemen's club. His best friend Randy, was recently assaulted by three men who pistol whipped him severely. After being released from the hospital, Deion asked Randy to celebrate his recovery by enjoying himself at the club. Deion told Randy that all lap dances would be free but Randy would still be required to pay the admission price at the door. An hour after Randy arrived at the club, Deion sent Randy a message and asked him to come downstairs for a surprise. After a few more lap dances, Randy walked to the basement to meet Deion. Randy was unaware that Deion captured the man who ordered the assault against him. When Randy entered the room, Deion yelled and said, "This is the coward who wanted you dead." As Randy quickly walked down the stairs towards the man who was tied by ropes while laying naked on top of a pool table, Randy tripped on a broken step. Unfortunately, Randy broke his ankle when he awkwardly fell to the floor.

To prevail if Randy sues Deion, which category best describes Randy?

(A) Non-Trespasser

(B) Invitee

(C) Trespasser

(D) Licensee

Notes

Question 61

The ACLU filed an action on behalf of local activist leaders in response to a police department running a helicopter surveillance program. This program used three helicopters to fly over the city during daytime hours, which captured hours of surveillance footage. The footage was used to assist in the prosecution of murders and many non-violent crimes. The ACLU filed a motion on behalf of leaders and argued that such governmental action violated the rights of citizens.

Will the ACLU prevail?

(A) Yes, due to a lack of probable cause, on the behalf of the police department.

(B) Yes, based on the Fourth Amendment.

(C) No, because of the Open-fields doctrine.

(D) No, based on an objective expectation of privacy, which is recognized by society and supported by the Constitution.

Notes

The Life

1. **C**

Future threats cannot be classified as being imminent threats. In order to use self-defense as a defense, reasonable force must be used to prevent a person from sustaining an imminent attack. Erica was not defending herself against an intentional tort or an imminent threat.

Notes

2. **A**

A delegator cannot escape liability, even if delegatees expressly assume the duties of the delegator. Moreover, a delegator cannot release him or herself from their contractual obligation, and is also secondarily responsible/liable for the performance, failure of performances of delegatees. Therefore, the contractor will be liable because of his responsibility to perform and Sam will remain secondarily responsible.

Notes

3. **B**

Congress can force states to obey certain conditions prior to receiving federal dollars. Federal funding can be attached with conditions, which Congress is allowed to do through its spending power. The United States Supreme Court has held that Congress is permitted to place conditions on federal funds, but the spending must serve the general welfare, the condition placed on the state must be unambiguous, the condition has to relate to the particular federal program, unconstitutional action cannot be a contingency of receipt of the funds, and the amount in question cannot be so great that it can be considered coercive to the state's acceptance of the condition.

Notes

4. **C**

A joint tenancy is a vehicle of concurrent ownership and it can involve two or more people who own property with a right of survivorship. In the context of a joint tenancy with a right of survivorship, if a living tenant devises their interest in the property, the devise will be ineffective because the death of one joint tenant will cause the deceased co-tenant's property interest to pass to the remaining joint tenant(s).

Notes

5. **C**

Under the Federal Rules of Evidence, 404(b), Evidence of other crimes, wrongs or acts is inadmissible to prove that a person acted in conformity with their character. However, evidence of other crimes, wrongs, or acts is admissible to prove motive, opportunity, intent, preparation, common plan or scheme, knowledge, identity or absence of mistake.

Notes

6. **D**

A demand for a jury trial must be made in writing and served within 14 days after the service of the last pleading, which is directed at the issue that is sought to be tried by a jury. A failure to file a demand for a jury trial in a timely manner is considered a waiver of a jury trial demand. Here, the jury trial demand was filed 22 days after the defendant's answer to the complaint.

Notes

7. **D**

Intentional dominion or control without permission involving personal property that is owned by someone else is conversion. Therefore, when Chris placed a drill inside of his jacket, he committed conversion.

Notes

8. **A**

Interpleader is applicable when two or more adverse parties seek ownership of the same thing, which is held by a third party. The property in question is called the stake, and the
party who has custody over the disputed stake is called the stakeholder. Interpleader permits the stakeholder to file an action against the adverse parties, which will require the adverse parties to litigate their claim of title between themselves, instead of litigating with the stakeholder.

Notes

9. **D**

According to the Federal Rules of Evidence, 1003; A duplicate copy of a contract is admissible to the same extent as the original contract, unless a question is raised concerning the authenticity of the original contract, or in the circumstances it would be unfair to admit the duplicate in lieu of the original contract. As such, because Veronica contested the authenticity of the original contract, and the original contract cannot be located, the court will not admit the duplicate contract into evidence.

Notes

10. **A**

Mootness will prevent a case from being dismissed if the injury suffered by the plaintiff is capable of being repeated, and will evade review by the courts if the case is dismissed. Here, because the policy regarding attire could arise for future students, the court will likely not dismiss the lawsuit.

Notes

11. **D**

A search warrant exception is the automobile search, which permits officers to search and seize items within an automobile where there is probable cause to believe the vehicle contains contraband. Once probable cause has been established, a police officer can search the entire vehicle, including closed containers. Therefore, the government can use this argument as grounds to justify the search of Lauren's entire vehicle.

Notes

12. **D**

Adverse possession allows a party to claim ownership of a property if their possession is: *open, actual, exclusive, hostile* and *continuous for the statutory period.*

Notes

13. **B**

When a person has committed a tortious act, subsequent injuries that arise from a rescue attempt are foreseeable. Moreover, a negligent rescue attempt is foreseeable. Generally, the tortfeasor who set the chain of tortious events into motion will be liable for injuries which are caused by a negligent rescuc attempt. Unforeseeable acts are considered superseding causes, such as subsequent intentional torts. However, negligence committed by intervening rescuers is foreseeable. Therefore, Sandy will be liable for Tom's extensive leg injuries.

Notes

14. **C**

Legislation concerning the health, safety and general welfare of the District of Columbia is regulated by Congress, according to Article 1, Section 8 of the Constitution.

Notes

15. **B**

Common law defines murder as an unlawful killing of another with malice aforethought. By Kareem pointing the gun at Nance's head and pulling the trigger, he acted with a reckless indifference concerning Nance's life.

Notes

16. **B**

The material aspect of a contract is based on certain conditions or circumstances that are vital concerning the proper completion of the contract. Express conditions are generally material and important aspects of contracts. When a party breaches such conditions, their breach will be considered a material breach. Such is the case with the African marble.

Notes

17. **A**

Diversity requires that opposing parties be from separate states, and the amount in controversy must exceed $75,000, excluding cost and interest. Here, the plaintiff is a citizen of state Q. The insurance company is a citizen of state M, its principal place of business was in state Q. A corporation is considered to be a citizen of the state where it is incorporated, and the jurisdiction where it has its principal place of business. Therefore, diversity is not satisfied and removal is not possible. Moreover, a lawsuit can only be removed to federal court if that lawsuit could have originally been filed in federal court.

Notes

18. **D**

An easement in gross specifically permits a person to access land which is owned by someone else.

Notes

19. **B**

A defendant's right to communicate with their attorney cannot be terminated by a Judge.

Notes

20. **D**

A temporary restraining order (TRO) can be granted without written or oral notice being provided to an adverse party. To do so, the plaintiff must articulate specific facts within a affidavit or within a verified complaint to reflect immediate and irreparable injury, loss, or damage that will occur to the applicant before the adverse party or that party's attorney can be heard in opposition. Also, the applicant's attorney must certify to the court in writing, the efforts, if any, which have been made to give the notice and the reasons supporting the claim that notice should not be required.

Notes

21. **A**

During an appeal, a party is prohibited from raising new issues or objections that were not raised during the trial, because trial courts must be granted the opportunity to rule on such issues.

Notes

22. **C**

Local municipalities establish the definition of zoning laws. In general, an industrial zoned area will include noise concerns. Industrial use such as manufacturing is typically not suitable, nor conducive for residential use.

Notes

23. **D**

Generally, a defendant can be held liable for intentionally or recklessly causing someone to experience severe emotional distress. A member of a victim's family can also recover damages, if a family member perceives the extreme or outrageous conduct, and the defendant knew or should have known that a family member was present, and would likely endure severe emotional distress from witnessing the defendant's conduct.

Notes

24. **C**

When a sufficient nexus exists between a seller and the state, where an item will be taxed, Courts will closely examine the nexus, including the interactions between a seller, the presence of their goods within the state, and the surrounding conduct of the seller concerning their efforts to make an item available within a state. This close inspection by the Court is used to determine the validity of a tax that is levied. Moreover, taxes can be imposed on items that do not presently exist within a state.

Notes

25. **C**

A document that existed prior to a person hiring an attorney will generally not be protected under the attorney-client privilege. However, when a client or attorney exchange written communications which relate to the client's representation, such written communication will generally be protected under the attorney-client privilege. Therefore, the attorney will be required to disclosed the personal bank account records of the CEO.

Notes

26. **C**

A total breach can be declared under the doctrine of anticipatory repudiation, if there is an unequivocal statement of unwillingness or an inability to perform a future contractual obligation. Because Sebastian told the auto shop that he could not make the $4,000 payment, the auto shop was permitted to treat the statement as a total breach.

Notes

27. **D**

Whenever a person kills someone during the commission or attempted commission of a serious or inherently dangerous crime, that person can be convicted of felony murder. The required mens rea is the intent to commit the underlining felony, which includes arson, rape, robbery or kidnapping. Felony murder also includes intentional and unintended killings. Therefore, because the defendant intended to commit a robbery, which resulted in the killing of Wally, the defendant can be convicted of felony murder.

Notes

28. **B**

When a jury reaches a verdict, the Court is permitted to poll the jury to determine if the verdict was unanimous. The verdict of a jury must be unanimous. However, if the verdict is not unanimous, the court can either order the jury to deliberate further or order a new trial.

Notes

29. B

When property is sold via foreclosure sale, the interest of junior lien holders will be wiped out. Yet, if a junior interest holder is not a party in the judicial proceeding concerning the foreclosure, and if the junior interest holder is not notified about the foreclosure sale, the interest of the junior lien holder will not be wiped out.

Notes

30. D

Lenoire could sue her boyfriend for being negligent, but that would be a long shot. However, Lenoire could not prove that her boyfriend teasing the defendant was the proximate cause of her injuries. Proximate cause requires that a plaintiff incur foreseeable harm, which is within the risk that is created by the conduct of the defendant. Here, it was not foreseeable that Lenoire would be shot as a result of her boyfriend teasing Miles.

Notes

31. D

The inchoate crime of conspiracy does not merge with the completed crime. Therefore, Larry can be convicted of conspiracy to commit jury tampering and jury tampering.

Notes

32. D

According to the 15th Amendment, U.S. citizens cannot be denied the right to vote, nor shall their right to vote be abridged by the United States or by any state on the account of race, color or a previous condition of servitude.

Notes

33. A

The doctrine of accord and satisfaction requires that the obligor to make a promise to accept some substituted performance, which will satisfy the obligee's original existing contractual duty. An accord requires mutual consideration. A substitute form of consideration can be satisfactory if the original owed duty is in doubt of being performed. Here, Billy and the mechanic shop owner agreed that a vehicle in good condition, with a clean title, could be a substitute for the $1,800 balance, although both forms of consideration are significantly different. Billy performed by delivering the truck, which represented the accord. Therefore, the mechanic shop owner will be forced to hold up his end of the deal, which will represent the satisfaction.

Notes

34. C

Under the Federal Rules of Evidence, 612, if a witness's memory is exhausted for any reason, the attorney performing the direct examination can attempt to refresh a witness's memory. However, procedural protections ensure that adverse parties are allowed to review writings that are used when the memory of a testifying witness is being refreshed.

Notes

35. D

The Free Exercise Clause cannot be used to challenge a law of general applicability unless it is revealed that the law was intended to interfere with religion. An individual cannot be punished by the government based on that individual's religious beliefs. Nevertheless, states are permitted to ban conduct on a general basis, even if that prohibition impedes a person's religious beliefs. Here, the amendment of the policy applied to all employees, regardless of individual religious beliefs. Therefore, Freddy's refusal to comply with the policy allows the hospital to deny benefits to Fredy's estate, without violating of the Free Exercise Clause.

Notes

36. C

If a defendant's presence in the forum state is based on force, fraud, or participation in some other judicial proceeding, the defendant will be exempt from being subjected to personal jurisdiction of that forum state.

Notes

37. D

Under the spousal testimony privilege, a witness spouse cannot be forced to testify against their spouse in a criminal proceeding. The spousal testimony privilege protects confidential communications made prior to and during the marriage from being admitted as evidence during a criminal trial.

Notes

38. B

The woman's mere presence was not enough to give the officers probable cause to search through the book bag. Even if officers seized the book bag, they would have to obtain a search warrant prior to searching through each bookbag. This is a huge distinction from the automobile search, which allows officers to search everywhere, including closed containers.

Notes

39. C

The United States Supreme Court has held that peremptory strikes cannot be used on the basis of race, ethnicity or sex.

Notes

40. A

The Fourth Amendment does not apply to immigration hearings.

Notes

41. B

Under the Federal Rules of Evidence, Rule 701, the opinion of a lay person is admissible concerning: (1) the general appearance or condition of a person; (2) the state of emotion of a person; (3) matters which involve sense recognition; and (4) identifying the likeness or identity of handwriting. Alternatively stated, the opinion of a lay person is admissible when such opinion is based on the witness's personal knowledge. Furthermore, the witness's testimony must be rationally based on the witnesses' perception and the testimony must be helpful to the trier of a fact, which is at issue. Therefore, the husband's testimony will be admissible because he observed Snow driving the car at a high rate of speed through the parking lot.

Notes

42. D

Congress is prohibited by the Tenth Amendment from interfering with the lawmaking processes of the states. Moreover, Congress cannot commandeer the states because states cannot be forced to execute federal programs.

Notes

43. B

Whenever goods are involved, the Uniform Commercial Code will apply. Under Article 2 of the UCC, a buyer can accept goods that are defective despite an improper executed tender. Acceptance has occurred when the buyer had an opportunity to inspect the goods, indicate their acceptance by informing the seller that the goods are in conformity with the terms of the contract, and the goods are accepted, despite any non-conformity, failing to make an effective rejection. Therefore, because Kevin had the opportunity but failed to inspect the flyers prior to the fifth day, his inaction will be treated as an acceptance.

Notes

44. B

Because the teenager entered the building with the intent of finding a place to sleep, without intending to cause harm to another person, the most serious crime that he can be charged with is trespass.

Notes

45. A

This auction was conducted "without reserve." As such, when the auctioneer opens the bidding process, his invitation to bid is treated as an offer, and the highest bid will be treated as accepting the auctioneer's offer. Consequently, Fatima's jewelry will be sold to the winner bidder, despite her protest.

Notes

46. A

Hilary's status transformed from an invitee to a trespasser when she went into the restricted area. Bill's sign, which warned customers not to go into the restricted area, was an exercise of reasonable care. As the owner of the premises, Bill had a duty to warn trespassers about hidden dangers that he was aware of.

Notes

47. B

Under the Federal Rules of Evidence, 405 (b), in cases where character or a character trait of a person is an essential element of a charge, claim or defense, proof of such character or a character trait can be proven by specific instances of conduct.

Notes

48. D

If an interested party has never had the opportunity to litigate an issue, that party cannot be halted by a finding in another party's case. Here, because the estate was not a party in the criminal prosecution of Hosea, the estate will not be estopped from bringing their wrongful death lawsuit.

Notes

49. A

Congress has a very broad scope of authority under the war power. Any course of action which is believed necessary to provide for the national defense, during war time and peace time is within the authority of Congress. Therefore, prohibiting the strike based on the tense circumstances would be considered an action that is within the interest of the national defense.

Notes

50. B

The United States Supreme Court has held that a person does not have a reasonable expectation of privacy regarding abandoned property. Under *Terry v. Ohio*, Investigatory stops by police officers are permitted if officers have reasonable suspicion, based on articulable facts that criminal activity is occurring or has occurred. Therefore, Jarod lost his expectation of privacy regarding the weapon upon throwing the item into the bushes.

Notes

51. A

The purpose of compensatory damages is to make the non-breaching party "whole" again. The measure of damages that are owed to a wrongfully discharged employee will be the agreed salary amount for the specified employment period. This measure of damage for a wrongfully discharged employee can be reduced by the amount the employee would have earned from obtaining comparable employment. Carlos was not in a position to mitigate his losses because there were no available similar employment opportunities. Therefore, John will be forced to pay Carlos the full salary amount of $40,000.

Notes

52. A

The classmate's freedom was not significantly deprived, meaning he was not placed in custody, nor was he a suspect, or subjected to a custodial interrogation. Therefore, the classmate's statements were given voluntarily, free of coercion or any circumstances which would require the detective to issue a Miranda warning.

Notes

53. D

Only Congress can formally declare war. However, the President can deploy troops without receiving congressional approval, but Congress can limit or expand the funding for troop deployment through Congress's spending power.

Notes

54. B

The offeree's (Maria) power of acceptance is terminated when he or she rejects the offeror's (Marshall) offer. An offeree's power of acceptance can be terminated in the following ways: *lapse of time, revocation by the offeror, rejection by the offeree, or death/incapacity.*

Notes

55. B

Because self-defense is an affirmative defense, a defendant will be required to prove self-defense by a preponderance of the evidence.

Notes

56. C

The First Amendment protects an individual's right to communicate their views with others. However, in order to justifiably restrict freedom of association, it must be proven that a person has joined an organization with the precise intent of advancing illegal activities. The First Amendment guarantees freedom concerning a person's right to assemble with others to express concerns regarding religion, politics and other topics, but in peaceful manner. However, in order to justifiably restrict the freedom of association, it must be proven that a person has joined an organization with the precise intent of advancing illegal activities.

Notes

57. D

Under the UCC, Section 2-201(2), when a contract is between merchants and one merchant sends a writing to the other, which confirms the contract within a reasonable time, and the receiving merchant is aware of the terms within the writing, but does not object to the writing within 10 days of receiving the writing, the writing will satisfy the Statute of Frauds. Here, 12 days passed and the wholesaler failed to object to the terms of the writing. Therefore, the letter sent by Phillip will satisfy the Statute of Frauds.

Notes

58. D

The credibility of a witness may be attacked by any party. Moreover, a witness can be proven to be bias, meaning he or she has a motivation to fabricate their testimony. Here, Hank's credibility can be attacked because he may be motivated to lie or exercise bias against Edward, due to Edward's romantic involvement with Hank's former girlfriend.

Notes

59. B

Unless a landlord agrees to a novation, the original tenant will not be released from contractual obligations that are owed to the landlord, based on the terms of the lease. Therefore, Thomas will prevail because the veterinarian is still obligated under the terms of the lease.

Notes

60. B

Randy is considered an invitee. The duty owed to an invitee involves exercising reasonable care, such as inspecting the property, discovering hidden and dangerous conditions, and protecting the invitee from such dangerous conditions.

Notes

61. B

The footage that was collected from the spy program would be considered fruit of the poisonous tree. Moreover, the Fourth Amendment was violated based on the persistent surveillance of outdoor movements, which invaded an individual's reasonable expectation of privacy.

Notes

Made in United States
North Haven, CT
27 June 2022